Hello, Yellow!

A Second Book of
Thought Provoking Poems

To Lri,

Enjoy!

Love.

Liz Mingo Liz Mingo

09/06/2023

Who Am I?

I was born in the Commonwealth of Dominica, West Indies. I came to England in 1975, a very shy 10 year old! I started writing in the late 80's after being prompted by a friend. I didn't take my writing seriously until much later. As I got older, my poems were influenced by events that were happening in everyday life, being reported on the news and issues experienced by family and friends. I would describe my poetry as a bag of liquorice allsorts - you will laugh, cry, think, start a debate, maybe even relate!

From my head, to my fingers, to the page, to your mind, to your body, to your soul!

I can be contacted on Instagram: @lizm4000.

Thank You

To my Family, nothing but Love, always.

To my Dearest Uncle Chicks, RIP. Yellow was your favourite colour too. Love & miss You!

To my Nephew Wesley. The coolest SEN Teen in MK. From weighing a pound at birth to a now super intelligent, handsome, 16 year old. You put the A in Able. Aunt Liz Loves You.

To my friends, thank you for the continued support.

A special Thank You to @Clovis.art21 for the inspiration.

Contents

1. Alone   1

2. As Clear as Day   2

3. The Black Woman   4

4. The Body   5

5. Broken   7

6. Colourless Gaze   8

7. A Confessional Poem (Falling in Love)   9

8. A Confessional Poem (Stealing a Kiss)   10

9. Connections   11

10. Crazy in Love   12

11. Daily Quote 1   13

12. Daily Quote 2   14

13. Daily Quote 3   15

14. Daily Quote 4   16

15. Daily Quote 5   17

16. Daily Quote 6   18

17. Dance   19

18. The Danger of You   20

19. Dear Diary   21

20. Do Not   23

21. Dream   24

22. Drink   25

23. Driving   26

24. Empty Bench   27

25. Erotica   28

26. Eureka!   29

27. Even   30

28. Falling...   31

29. Falling for You   32

30. Finding Love   33

31. Fine on the Outside   34

32. Giving Them a Voice   35

33. The Gun that Wanted to Be a Lamb   37

34. Hands Up   38

35. Heartbreak   39

36. Hush   40

37. I Called It Love   41

38. I Put Our Love in a Box   42

39. I Wish   43

40. Infectious   44

41. Is It Love?   45

42. Journey   46

43. Last Night   47

44. Lessons from Mother   48

45. Men-Tal Health   49

46. A Mile in My Shoes   50

47. The Miles Between Us   51

48. More   52

49. My Hands Are Tied   53

50. My Skin   54

51. A Picture   55

52. Poets in a Corner   56

53. Reaching Out   57

54. Reveal   58

55. River   59

56. Romantic Relations   60

57. Secrets   61

58. See the Able, not the Label   62

59. Shackled   63

60. Slow Motion   64

61. Smile   65

62. A Spell Poem (Words into Flesh)   66

63. Thank You!   68

64. That Thing!   69

65. Touch   70

66. Trance   71

67. A Transformational Poem (a Gun)   72

68. Travel with Me   73

69. Unsaid Words   74

70. Venice   75

71. What Happens Next   76

72. What Stops You   77

73. Wild Thoughts   78

74. Words   79

Alone

She lies there
Motionless
Red silky sheets pulled low to her buttocks
Revealing a perfect hourglass figure
Naked
Like the day she was born
Hands caress her entire body
Moving slowly
From shoulders down, and back again
Sweetness tinged with pain...
The hands are her own
A creature of such beauty
Yet she's alone
That in itself is a mystery!

As Clear as Day

[Trigger warning: self-harm]

I remember.
I remember the day.
I see it even when I'm not looking.
I remember.
Etched in some part of my brain,
It never leaves.
Do I want it to?
I remember
I held the knife against my wrist,
Longed to press down on it
To no longer exist...
I remember
Wanting to see blood,
Didn't want to keep breathing.
Compos mentis.
Even of sound mind
I wanted to do this,
Slit my wrists.
I remember
The day my mother took her last breath
In August 1984.
I remember that day
Like it was yesterday!
So long ago

Yet still so raw.
Sheer trauma.
I remember
'Cause I wanted to die too!

The Black Woman

We are what you see
Black, Beauty
Our hair
Long and flowing; or
Short, twisted kinks; or
Sometimes locked; and
No, you cannot touch!
Our Mona Lisa smiles
Our hips, gyrating from side to side even without music!
Our well-rounded butts
Our golden complexions
The perfect ingredients
To generate admiration
We so darn sexy
I see you checking me
Naturally
I fit into this category

The Body

OMG,
Is that really me?
Should have avoided the mirror!

Okay, so you may not believe it,
But once upon a time I was well fit.
In fact, I had a six-pack.
Think it's time to get that body back!
Gonna need to be disciplined,
Tuck that tummy in, and eat the right things.

So out go the Twix, Maltesers, Snickers bars.
In fact, no more chocolate...
I'm already beginning to hyperventilate.

But, no pain, no gain as they say.
It's a brand-new day,
So, let's do this!

First off, hire a PT
Who will motivate me,
And set up my low-calorie
Eating plan.
In no time I'll be back to my old self:
Faster, stronger, fitter and in super health!

I'll be glowing from my head to my toes
And be able to fit into my old clothes.

Can't wait!
What absolute bliss
To be back to 36-24-36,
And wearing my figure-hugging outfits.

No more Miss Piggy jokes.
Instead, back to wolf whistles from the blokes!
I'll have my old body back,
Walking down the street, showing off,
Strutting my stuff.

Okay, enough of this dream, let's make it reality.
But first, one last chocolate frenzy!

Broken

I'm in pieces
My heart is broken
Lost my love and I'm not sure how, or why
I would cry
But I have no tears left

Colourless Gaze

I have eyes only for you
So full of admiration
But you don't look at me the same
Your gaze is blank, colourless
And instantly, my heart is broken

A Confessional Poem (Falling in Love)

Can't deny how much I'm liking this!
I'm complete
Can't put a time on when
But when doesn't matter
It's the here, and now
Love this feeling
Of being...

A Confessional Poem (Stealing a Kiss)

But if it had to be stolen from anyone
It would have to be you
So, with your face up close and personal
My eyes were firmly on the prize
It was now or never
Didn't ever
Have myself down as a pilferer
But life's not always fair
So, with the swiftness of a tigress
I go in for the kill
Facing my direction
I pounce!
Touchdown
My work here is done

Connections

It's said that people come into our lives for a reason
Whatever that reason may look like
Some reasons are as simple as locking eyes
Be it in a crowded room
Or on a busy commute
Some connections stick, and last a lifetime
Others fizzle out before even taking off
Some connections may have you falling in love
For whatever reason, people come into our lives

Crazy in Love

How does one know when one is not just in love, but
Crazy in love!
Thinking about them every second of every day
Wondering what they're doing
Where they are
Who they're with
Fixation?
Obsession?
Crazy?
Or crazy in love?
Perhaps all of the above!

Daily Quote 1

You may not understand it
But it's happening
You try to connect the dots
Somehow it still doesn't add up
But does that matter?
Who says everything has to make sense?

Daily Quote 2

There's always a way out
No matter what
It may not seem that way
While you're in the mêlée
But every entrance has an exit
So look for it

Daily Quote 3

Everyone has something that's a pull to someone else.
What may be attractive to you may not be attractive to me.

Daily Quote 4

If you woke up today
Be grateful
Seize the moment
Carpe diem!
No rewind, 'cause it's not a movie
No rematch, 'cause it's not a game
This is life, so live it
'Cause when it's gone, it's gone!

Daily Quote 5

Sometimes we wake up smiling
Other times we wake up crying
Sometimes we wake up with no clear vision
But it's all good
It reminds us that we're human
These feelings are natural
And they will pass
If we've been given another day
Be thankful and embrace it
'Cause once we have life, we can change the narrative

Daily Quote 6

What more does one need
To be motivated?
You're alive
Another day to thrive
Go! Go! Go!

Dance

We hit the dance floor
Arms firmly placed around my waist
You pull me in
We jive to the beat
Instant body heat
My heart's pounding
Sweat's pouring
C'est magnifique
Encore! Encore!
We tap our feet
Ready, set, go...
Next up, *la danse de l'amour*
My body's on fire
And wanting more, more, more!

The Danger of You

It's not that you're dangerous,
It's the vibes you give off:
The glances in my direction
Making my nipples stand to immediate attention!
The way you smell
I know it so well,
That even in an unlit room
You ignite me.

Dear Diary

Here are the day's secrets,
Which I trust you'll keep
Under lock and key
By remaining tightly shut!

You know my innermost thoughts,
Every nook and cranny,
From the guys I wanna marry
To those I just wanna FUCK!

You know the people I love
And those I don't give a shit about,
The ones I trust
And those who piss me the hell off!

You know the bitches!
The ones who pretend to be friends
But are really just acquaintances.
They get on my last nerve!

The ones who act like they like you
When in fact, what they truly want to do,
Is take your man!

Dear Diary,
We're in this together.
I know you, you know me.
Protect my privacy. And
Thank you for allowing me to write so candidly!

I do not doubt your loyalty,
But please do not mention my lewd acts,
Otherwise, I'll invest in a Filofax!

Thank you.

Yours indebtedly,
ME!

Do Not

I am a voice in this world
And I deserve to be heard
All day, every day
So, do not only acknowledge me
During Black History Month
Take heed of what I have to say
I am just as important as you
Therefore, my words carry weight too
Am I that different?
My race? I am who I am
My face? It has its own gloss
I do not need you to repaint it
I simply need you to acknowledge me
So, if actions speak louder than words then prove it
Show me that you are listening!

Dream

Been having this dream
It's me meeting you, meeting me
You get down on one knee...
I already know what my answer will be
Can't wait till this becomes reality!

Drink

I appreciate you may be thirsty,
But do not rush me.
Look at this body,
Fully matured, like a fine wine.
I should not be gulped,
But instead,
Drank sparingly, a sip at a time...

Driving

Have I told you lately
That you're driving me crazy!
Well you are.
But it's okay,
'Cause Baby,
I wouldn't want it any other way!
You take my breath away.

Empty Bench

It has such character
Like no other
A multitude of bums have sat
And reminisced
About being kissed
Right here, on this seat

Erotica

Ice cubes on a naked body
Nothing more erotic
Positioning is key of course
Just below the breasts
Directly on the belly button, and
Just between the thighs
With eyes firmly on the prize
Mouth to cube
Moving slowly, in a circular motion
First clockwise, then anti
Until each one melts to the groans of ecstasy!

Eureka!

Thoughts of you
Awaken dormant senses
My body's on a high
Fingers caress my inner thighs
I'm a window shopper
You're the cherry popper
Try to speak, but
I'm tongue-tied
Knees all weak
Body on heat
Beads of sweat
Bed's all...

Oh shucks!
Another wet dream

Even

Why do I even care?
The question is constant
I look at you, and the feeling is instant
But why the hell do I even care!
You're grown
Do grown-up stuff
Yet a diamond in the rough
A rare gem
Rough at the edges and needing guidance
But it's really not my place
I should keep the hell away
So why the hell do I even care?
I love you, that's why!

Falling...

In a room full of people,
Yet the only face I want to see is yours.
So many voices,
Yet the only voice I want to hear is yours.
Think I've fallen...
Hook, line and sinker.

Falling for You

Purely platonic is what we agreed,
And I've really tried to respect that.
Hadn't expected this 360,
But now you've gripped me
Like a good movie.
Can no longer resist,
So, may we change the script?
It's just that, I'm falling for you.

Finding Love

Minding my own business,
Walking down the street.
Wasn't expecting it,
What happened next,
But there you were,
Totally by surprise.
You caught my eye,
Took my breath away.
And just like that, I ended up finding love!

Fine on the Outside

No one sees the tears I cry
Because I cry internally
I'm an emotional mess
But who'd guess?
I put on a brave face
But don't know why
All this bravery shows I'm fine on the outside
But my insides are paying the price!

Giving Them a Voice

[Trigger warning: Abuse]

To all those who fit under this umbrella
I apologise
My eyes
Are blinded with tears
That you were subjected to such cruelty
And
Most probably
By those who should have protected
Those who should have been your safety net
And yet
They let you fall
Every sinew
Shattered
Broken
However, your truth needs to be spoken
So if your tongue is heavy
I give you my voice
Use it! Use me!
Tell your story
To the world, and then some
I appreciate you may feel alone – don't!
I stand with you
I walk with you
I hold your hand

Two voices are better than one
So, with yours and mine, NO MORE
No more silence!
Say it loud. Say it clear!
Let every abuser hear
You survived
NO MORE disguising
NO MORE hiding
NO MORE!
From here on in
You're SURVIVING!

The Gun that Wanted to Be a Lamb

For the most part I'm respected, held in high regard
But I long to be something else
Not wanting all this publicity and bad press
If I asked the question you'd not guess
In a million years what I truly long to be
This is heartbreak for me!
I'm so unhappy with who I am
A piece of machinery, a tool
Can't help that I'm a firearm (I get that)
But I'd prefer my legacy not to be about causing harm
I detest being used as a scapegoat
(Or any goat for that matter!)
Oh to be revered, sheared, considered sacred
I'd rather pump milk than bullets
I'd even take being the main ingredient in a tasty casserole
or Sunday roast
Sure, I'd be dead then, but at least
I would have been a lamb!

Hands Up

Okay, you've caught me.
I'm in that moment of rapture.
Sheer pleasure.
What utter joy!
My tongue acts as a toy,
A comforter to suck on!
If you could see my eyes,
They would not tell lies.
Even my body language says:
Relaxed.

Heartbreak

Never believed heartbreak was visible
Until it landed at my door
Literally came out of my chest
And splattered on the floor
It wasn't hidden anymore!

Hush

Hand to mouth
Restricting speech
Fingers caress lips
Moist to the touch
Adrenalin rush
Unadulterated crush
Fantasy ignited
Love requited
Speech uninvited
Shhhhhhh...
Hand to mouth
Silence demanded!

You've caught me in the moment of climax!

I Called It Love

I called it love and you said it was a misunderstanding
How did I get it so twisted?
Not even on the same page
After all we shared
All the intimate moments
They felt so real!
But clearly not for you
I'm lost and brokenhearted
But understand this: Go to hell!

I Put Our Love in a Box

What we have is so precious
This love
Like crowned jewels
Many are jealous
Eyes so fixed on us
It scares me that I may lose you
And, though selfish,
I put our love in a box
And secured it with locks
With combinations only I know

I Wish

I'm kicking myself!
Can't believe I just let you go
Without even saying hello
There you were, right in front of me
Those eyes! Those lips!
That physique...
All left me speech...less!
An opportunity missed.
... I wish
I could turn back time

Infectious

Like a disease on the skin
Spreading like wildfire
I'm hot to the touch
Temperature rising by the second
From this infection
Think me crazy, but I'm happy to be infected some more
Doesn't attack everyone, just me
He's my disease and I'm not looking for a cure!

Is It Love?

Is it love that has me so weak
I cannot eat or sleep
Is it love that has me doing the strangest things?
Is it love that has me tongue-tied?
Or do I want this so badly
I'm letting it consume me?
Is it love?
Was it ever love?
Maybe just the thought of being in love

Journey

The journey back to you
Has been my best journey yet!

Last Night

So, about last night...
Was it good for you?
It was for me!
Tell me honestly
'Cause if we both enjoyed it
Can we hit repeat?

Lessons from Mother

Be respectful
Be grateful
Lead, do not follow
Be thankful, even for the little things
Stay grounded
Inspire
Give willingly
Love
Always 'do you'
'Cause no one else can!

Thanks Mum!

Men-Tal Health

Make no excuses
Embrace your fight
Navigate your way
Through this battle
And find a solution to
Lessen the stereotype

Help is there, so seek it
End the stigma and misbelief
And allow men to share their grief
Let them inhale, and exhale, and
Tell their stories freely, 'cause the
Hype about Men-Tal Health is real!

A Mile in My Shoes

I dare you!
I double dare you!
Walk a mile in these shoes, my shoes!
Not a challenge one would choose
If the truth of my journey were
Known to all and sundry
So why judge me
From behind closed eyes
Dark glasses
Joining forces with the masses
Glaring disrespect!
A mile would not be enough
To truly reflect
The steps
I have taken
These shoes may look new
Trendy and branded
But they do not put my life in full view
And if those who judge had the slightest clue
They could not walk half an INCH in MY shoes!

The Miles Between Us

We tried
Oh how we tried
The sleepless nights
Crying, trying, crying some more
But the outcome was inevitable
That, we knew for sure!
We gave it our best shot
Yet that wasn't enough...
The miles between us are far too great!

More

Vous et moi
Je t'aime
Mon amour
You leave me wanting more
Our lovemaking
So hot and steamy
Our kisses
So wet and sultry
Our bodies
Forever intertwined
Burning with passion
Skin to skin
Exploring...
You leave me wanting more

My Hands Are Tied

I'd love to, but my hands are tied
And for that, I do apologise
However, if the final decision was mine,
I'd say yes, Yes, YES every time!

My Skin

My skin is just a coating
It does not define me
Or my personality
It is golden brown
A tone that makes many frown
Judging me by the colour of my skin
This old chestnut is wearing thin
Look beyond it, into my heart
Better to judge me by what's in that!

A Picture

If my eyes could take a picture
They would snap you
Said picture would be framed
With my name
Etched across your face
It would sit on my mantelpiece
Have pride of place
I'm liking this vision...
Smile!

Poets in a Corner

We come together
Bound by an embrace
Cheek to cheek

We kiss

How I long to stay in this place
This moment
With you. Do you, with me?

The pounding of your heart tells me this
So I question no more
We truly want the same things
To remain as we are, in this moment
Even if all around us should start to crumble
We shall know nothing about it
We are in heaven
Me into You equals paradise

Lovers
Poets in a corner
Ready to write the next
Chapter

Reaching Out

Arms outstretched
As far as they will go
As wide as an ocean
Do you see them?
More importantly, do you see me?
I'm reaching out with such hope
Will you at least meet me halfway?

Reveal

Tell your darkest secrets
Let them be your moon
Take off all your masks
Said cracks are yours
Let them see all of you
If they choose to walk
It is their loss
Be true to you

River

My love flows like a river
Through my bloodstream
My every thought
Praying that the force of gravity
Will lead me to you
With arms stretched out wide
And feelings running deep
Wading through until we meet!

Romantic Relations

Whatever the dynamic
Being in a relationship
Leaves you open to so many emotions
Vulnerability probably tops that list
The head, the heart, the mind, the body – all exposed
Not all relationships end, or end badly
On the contrary
A relationship can be a beautiful thing
Some run their course, and others
Simply run out of steam
Still, better to have loved...?

Secrets

I have many
But sadly, can't reveal any
However, if I had to
Hands down
My best kept secret would be you!

See the Able, not the Label

He's super intelligent
Mad about music
A gadget junkie
He has ADHD, many other complications
And autism
Nothing gets pass him
So
Never reveal your pin
Not to your phone, iPad, laptop – anything!
He never forgets a number
And though he's a statistic
And on a list
To me, the only labels he carries are
His name and 'nephew'
He puts the A in Able
Wes, Wes – Aunt Liz loves you!

Shackled

They shackled her body, but not her spirit
No number of chains could break that
Her spirituality kept her intact
Made her mentally strong
Prayer too was her companion
She knew this couldn't last forever
Nothing would deter her
Her body may have taken a beating, but she would never
give in

Slow Motion

My hand
        Glides
            Across
                The
                        Page
                  Without
              Rage
          Or
  Direction
        'Cause
              I'm
                  Writing
               In
                  Slow
                     Motion!

Smile

I love your smile!
Certainly lights up a room
Bright enough to make flowers bloom
Can never get enough – of you or it
Camera is in focus...
Please SMILE, I'm about to click!

A Spell Poem (Words into Flesh)

Many a spell has been attempted
I'm uncertain of past successes
However, I'll try now: my own potion
To win your love and devotion
Will it be hit or miss?
Will it see us locking lips?

First a ganache, chocolate and cream
Then a splash of olive oil goes in
Raw cabbage and carrots
Then a sprinkling of nuts

Second, a shot of whisky
Which surely will render us frisky
And make my body tremble
So another shot to the potion

Then I whisk, and I stir
And I stir and I whisk
Each time more rapid

I stop!

With eyes shut, I take a swig
Now for the big reveal...

Well blow me down
I've ended up with a salad
Quite yummy I might add!

Thank You!

I don't say this enough
But thank you so much
For all you've done and continue to do
I wouldn't be the person I am
If you hadn't taken the time
To love and nurture and instil
Your words of wisdom

That Thing!

That one thing
That one time
Now a lasting memory!

Touch

You're beautiful!
May I touch you?
Your face, your eyes, your lips
I will not stop until you say
So please
Play dumb
While I continue to work my way down...

Trance

You had me dazed
And in a trance
The moment you made your entrance
On my hands and knees, like a lovesick puppy
Tail wagging profusely
Waiting, with anxious (im)patience
For the signal to jump up
And start licking your face off!

A Transformational Poem (a Gun)

Bang!

        Bang!

                Bang!

Oh dear, fingers have woken me
I sincerely hope they have read the handbook
Of my every nook
About how I should be operated
I certainly can't be underestimated
I can cause harm in the right hands
Much less the wrong ones!
Caution must be observed each time I'm touched
There should be no rush
To want to own me or members of my family – AK47,
Pistol, Rifle, Smith & Wesson
We should be left well alone!
However, it's fair to say, I'm here to stay
Although I'm taken advantage of, there are uses for me
Least of all being used as a ploy, to scare
But don't be mistaken, I'm no toy
I do not release water, I deploy
Bullets!

Travel with Me

I long to get away
But to no specific place
So, without knowing where
Will you travel with me?

Unsaid Words

You're in pain
But say nothing
Your face is a picture
Of unpleasantries
That can't be hidden
But speech is forbidden!
You're sad
Your sadness is visible
In everything you do
But there's no one to listen
So your sadness remains unspoken
It's tough
But keep positive
Be strong
Stay true
Every dog has its day
Soon, you too will bark
And Unsaid Words will be a thing of the past

Venice

You and me
In Venice
So romantic
City of water
A trip on the gondola
Italy, *bellissimo!*
Ice creams and *cornetto*
But what I didn't know
Is what you had in store
When you got on the floor
And shouted "*Sposami!*"
My response was instant –
"*Certo! Ti amo!*"

What Happens Next

I remember it so clearly,
The day we met.
It was cold and wet,
But despite the storm,
My heart was warm.
What happened next?
We fell in love!

What Stops You

What stops you from loving me?
Am I not attractive enough?
Don't fit nicely into your box?
I'm smart, can hold a convo, opinionated, and financially
stable
I bring so much to the party
So what stops you from loving me?

Wild Thoughts

These thoughts!
So wild I should not even think them
Yet I find myself doing just that
They hit like a motherfucking heart attack!
It's the element of surprise
I look into those eyes
And oh, these wild thoughts
All-consuming and hot
Like NesCaff
I try not to drink while hot
But damn
Hard to resist
I push to the side
And allow to cool
Sip, sip, sip
These wild thoughts have me licked!

Words

Black and blue,
Yet I have not fallen!
Sticks and stones
May break my bones
You may be pleasured by my groans
But words alone will not dent
And will not cause me to vent
So avert your anger elsewhere
It is not welcomed here
Your abuse falls on deaf ears
I refuse to shed tears
Black defines me, it is my race
So perhaps blue
Is a reflection of YOU?